GREG DELANTY was born in Cork, Ireland in 1958, and now lives for most of the year in America, where he teaches at St Michael's College, Vermont. He has received numerous awards, including the Patrick Kavanagh Award, the Allan Dowling Poetry Fellowship, and the Austin Clarke Centenary Poetry Award. In 1999 he was a prizewinner in the National Poetry Competition. He has received an Irish Arts Council bursary, and has been widely anthologised.

T0148924

Also by Greg Delanty

Poetry Collections
Cast in the Fire
Southward
American Wake
The Hellbox
The Blind Stitch

Special Poetry Editions
The Fifth Province
Striped Ink

Translations
Aristophanes, The Suits (originally *The Knights*)
Euripides, Orestes

Edited
Jumping Off Shadows: Selected Contemporary Irish Poets
(with Nuala Ní Dhomhnaill)
The Selected Poems of Patrick Galvin
(with Robert Welch)

GREG DELANTY

The Ship of Birth

OxfordPoets

CARCANET

Acknowledgements

American Scholar, De Braake Hond, C-Span2: Poets Against the War, Contemporary Poetry of New England, Cry Out: Poets Protest the War, Foilsiu, Helicon, London Poetry Review, Metre, Natural Bridge, OnEarth, Partisan Review, Poetry Daily, Poetry Ireland Review, The Recorder, The Shop, Southern Review, Times Literary Supplement, TriQuarterly.

First published in Great Britain in 2003 by
Carcanet Press Limited
Alliance House
Cross Street
Manchester M2 7AQ

A CIP catalogue record for this book is available from the British Library
ISBN 1 903039 63 0

The publisher acknowledges financial assistance from Arts Council England

Typeset in Monotype Janson by XL Publishing Services, Tiverton
Printed and bound in England by SRP Ltd, Exeter

Contents

For Daniel especially

Lie still in thy berth
and I'll log the days
of your arrival – may
my words
be lanugo-soft
for fear
they turn you
away.

The Alien

I'm back again scrutinising the Milky Way
　　　　of your ultrasound, scanning the dark
　　　　　　　　matter, the nothingness, that now the heads say
　　　　is chockablock with quarks & squarks,
gravitons & gravitini, photons & photinos. Our sprout,

who art there inside the spacecraft
　　　　of your ma, the time capsule of this printout,
　　　　　　　　hurling & whirling towards us, it's all daft
　　　　on this earth. Our alien who art in the heavens,
our Martian, our little green man, we're anxious

to make contact, to ask divers questions
　　　　about the heavendom you hail from, to discuss
　　　　　　　　the whole shebang of the beginning&end,
　　　　the pre-big-bang untime before you forget the why
and lie of thy first place. And, our friend,

to say Welcome, that we mean no harm, we'd die
　　　　for you even, that we pray you're not here
　　　　　　　　to subdue us, that we'd put away
　　　　our ray guns, missiles, attitude and share
our world with you, little big head, if only you stay.

Today's light would break the hearts of the dead
        if they could step back in.
The sun filters through the lightest haze, a gauze
        of light
swabbing eye-cataracts that shroud what must be
        spirit-eyes.

It's as if the sun is seen through Japanese rice paper
        laid over
a timeless print or poem, suggesting core light
        that the sketch,
or calligraphy leaves out so the essence blazes
        through
– what the ghosts might call the divine, that may
        be seen only at one remove.

Or, as now, at one remove through this haze's tracing
        paper, the kind that as kids we simply
traced the sun, clouds, water, trees, people, cars
        and boats of our crayon-colourful world through.
As it is now and never again shall be: fawn-fall grass,
        the milkweed-seeded air, the vermilion trees,
the lake's veiled boats, the ghost of a passing truck
        and the gray scribble
on this paper white as a wimple, lit up as if from
        inside
by the unseen grand hand on this day that breaks
        the heart of a man gone all simple.

The kith and kin souls of those who've gone hover
      above the couple making love, elbow into
the woman's underworld, drinking the man's buttermilk
      in their ghostly death-drought, to recast our ilk.
Welcome Mona, Olla Anna Lopes Ferreira, and you
      Rob, and all the Danny Boys. I could go on forever
invoking the dead. Each clamouring chromosome
      roll-calls out of the past, at home
          in this character small enough to set down
      within the palm of my hand. Our dust-come-to-life,
whose antique eyes have you? Whose frown?
      Whose disposition? Whose strain of strife?
We toast you now, our ancient child risen from the tomb,
kidnapped by a band of ghosts, bound in your dark room.

The percolator is a gurgling alembic
     brewing the morning's spluttering slick.
I bask in the coffee's simple balm.
        For once I'll be wise and forgo
        turning to the company of the radio,
        the world's hourly news and see
        if the goldfinch and the chickadee
          will come to our feeder,
        to our coffee-brown sunflower seed.
I'll accept the responsibility of being calm.
I'll pay attention to the small creatures,
     to their broadcast and specific morning need.
     This morning I will pay special heed.

Sonogram

Now it's like a flashlight fanned down into the dark
        you've landed in,

not unlike a cross-section of the light wedge
revealing the missing child after the toddler
        wandered off from the picnic
        and the ground opened up
            burying him alive
            in the escape vault
        of an abandoned mine.

Each parent faulting the other.

                    *

When the doctor points to the white hole,
        the screen's bright nebula,
and matter-of-factly mouths words
            we can't understand,
except for *possible chromosome abnormality*,
        I thought of that drinking spree night
about the time we gave up on hitting the jackpot
        of you, our mite –
Next day I heard your mother sigh
            in a guest house bathroom
                as the EPT popsicle stick
                turned a stop-light red.

The doctor's words
            recalled the hangover pallor
            of her face.
    They settle in her stomach like lead.

Our newly found mummy in a crypt,
         so fragile that even a mere gust
                  must turn you to dust,
I knock on wood now for you
                  in your birth box,
that we'll only have to welcome you
         into the school of normal hard knocks.

Sound Kinetics

It dawned on me as we woke to Manhattan's sea-sound
        of traffic, how this is akin to what you hear,
pressed like an ear to the shell of your mother,
            unable to match sound to moving bodies.

I could tell you, since the doctors say you can
        distinguish voices and we must converse with you,
that the scraping of a steel ladder telescoping up
            the walls outside our window, heavenward,

is secure, and that the window cleaner
        works our window into an angel's sudsy wings
before he whistles to the top storey and climbs off
            to loll away the day on cloud nine;

that the hammering is a cavil playfully
        demanding everyone on the street be quiet
to allow the sidewalk magician to saw
            a street volunteer in half; or

that the soft moans of a woman and man
        is a couple making out. These are, of course,
all hypotheses, conjectures of sound;
            tall noise without a hint

of the window cleaner's drudgery,
        the carpenter's impatience, the traffic
that is more a tinnitus than a calming susurrus,
            and, a white lie for another reason entirely,

that the moaning – which, by the way,
        has stopped now – was a couple next door
and not, of course, your ma & da. This is no more
            than an exposé on the kinetics of love.

Sighting

All week I've been out of kilter, down in the dumps
  for no apparent reason.
Perhaps, I'd simply been too balanced, happy even,
  and the old roller-coaster
god of humour, Doctor Mood-Swinger himself, has said
  'Enough.
You're gettin' under my skin. Old boy, it's time for
  your general depression shot.'

*

Now it's mid-morning and I still can't get going. I potter
  round the house
and say alright, so be it, welcome Mr Down, Mr
  Nightday, old faithful companion.

*

No sooner do I shake hands with Squire Black and we get
    all chummy,
inseparable even, than this pair of goldfinch perch on either side
    of our pendulum feeder.
One's the yellowest yellow I have ever laid eyes on,
    the other's an off-yellow.
They are my selves: the upbird and the off-yellow
    downbird, balancing the fulcrum.
I look up. The birds take off out of sight into summer-thick air.
    Soon enough
I'll be out of here myself. Soon enough. That's alright now though.
    That's alright.

The Expected

You've been lying low, keeping mum
        of late. On coveted nights, our chum,
your mother and I have forgotten
        you're there, settling into our routine,
on the lam from quotidian strife:
        money worries, the brandished knife
in an e-mail, the hell-for-leather
        workaday world, the lousy weather.
Perhaps you've sensed what lurks outside
        and decided simply to hide
the way creatures do before a storm,
        their antennae sensing harm.
Have you picked up how we're slow
        to relinquish the world that we forego
to have you, our sulking mouse? You see,
        your mother and I are not unhappy
alone together. Do you understand?
        Many a day we are grand,
simply chatting with one another,
        spoofing away bother.
Chitmouse, it's impossible to explain
        our lives before your reign.
It's as if we're quietly dying
        and know it, wondering
at our terminal time, coveting the last
        haven weeks as they trimester past.
But for your sake I'll say no more.
        Mum's the word now, a stór.

When the squadrons of night-dropped parachutists
        on D-Day were scattered far and wide
        across the occupied French countryside,
finding themselves suddenly alone in forests,
        swamps and fields swarming with the Hun,
they had these thingamajig hand crickets,
        clickers you get in Christmas stockings.
Searching in the dark to hook up with their own,
        they'd cricket code clickclack clickclack
hearing a rustle of movement, footsteps approaching,
        waiting for the responding cricket greeting.
Tonight, little cricket, unable to hack
        news of another war, I came out to our garden
        and had nothing, nothing to cricket-call you back.

Later tonight
it's to turn cold, the old sudden sharp
        iceberg cold of New England.
Crickets, cicadas, grasshoppers and frogs
        play on.
What their songs and wing-music are saying,
        I can't say,
except they must know already that the ice
        has gashed a gaping hole
in the hull of Indian Summer and they
        are the quartet
that comes out on deck and plays away
        as the great ship goes down.
We listen quietly from our deck's lifeboat.
        Play on
brave, noble souls. Play on. *Nearer, my God,*
        to thee. Nearer to thee.

Squadrons of geese fall-fly south, moving in
      and out of rank,
honking simply to stay together and to swap
      leader.
The teachers urge the children to look at fighter
      jets, the Thunderbirds,
a name taken from the great Indian bird, but
      nothing is said of that provenance.
The new god rips open the tepee vault of the
      sky above our schools and homes.
No one points out the caret of geese inserting
      themselves peacefully on the day,
or mentions what exactly the Thunderbirds, awesome
      and all as they are, mean to insert.
The geese unravel their chevron ranks, their echelon
      formation and, as if in civil disobedience,
reform again, but this time into a child's copybook
      correct sign.

The Sea Horse Family

The sea horse is a question-mark in the ark of the ocean
        that's carried it without question all this way.
Mythical as a unicorn, and even less believable
        with its dragon head, its body a legless horse
                perpetually rearing, its monkey tail
        anchoring it to sea grass, sponge or coral,
but, my mate,
        no stranger than who you are to yourself,
        feeling large as a whale and small as a human.
Today I'd have us become sea horses, and I,
        being the male, would be the one in the family way.
I'd lug our hippocampus, our capall mara, our shy sea pony,
        our question-mark anchored in you,
unquestionably unfurling its self day by tidal day.

Most people are caught up in the snow-mobbed day.
            Some are even ecstatic, the snow
                        is still, after all, a novelty, a show
                                    getting under way.
Others are already dismayed,
            cursing impassable streets, traffic delayed
                        and the general disarray
of winter giving itself its own ticker tape parade.

The Shutterbug

'The day I developed the negative of a snowflake made by this method and found it
good, I felt like falling on my knees and worshipping it.'
          Wilson 'Snowflake' Bentley, Jericho, Vermont, 1885

I want to be a kind of Snowflake Bentley.
After years of standing out in the below zero
weather of Jericho and neighbours declaring him
off the wall, chasing snow chimeras,
he finally caught a crystal and another and
another, invisible white flowers blooming
in the illusory snow desert of winter,
stars whose light has only just become visible,
asterisks footnoting the flaky mystery.
He recalled the Eskimo notion that snowflakes are souls
that descend and enter the expecting mother
and creep into the child's body.
                            And now, our snowdrop,
since your body's all there and the first snow
is falling, softly falling on the world outside
our window, laying out its own carpet
maybe to welcome your soul-star, your soul-flower,
your soul-asterisk into your body, maybe even now
as your mother steps out on the walkway
to fetch the recycling bin. Farfetched, right enough,
but I peer through our blind as determined
as Snowflake behind his camera's curtain,
a snatcher of snowflakes, to catch
your soulflake, the forecasted simplicity below
the whole show. I pray, as Bentley prayed
over a fresh crystal, that your flake holds,
that you're not one of those flimsy drops, but rather
a fur-flake, snug and at home as a fur-coated Eskimo
stepping out of your igloo into the universe of snow.

The Soul Hunter

'The Tongans imagined the human soul to be the finer or more aeriform part of the body... something comparable to the perfume or essence of a flower as related to the more solid vegetable fiber.'
Edward Burnett Tylor, *Religion in Primitive Culture,* 1958

People have their smells too,
indefinable odours,
individual
as a fingerprint;
how I spirit-whiff
the redolence in homes
beside coffee, dinner, diaper and other
somatic pot-pourri odour;

how a girlfriend
has a sweet scent
– a spirit balm
beyond birds' & bees' endorphin beckoners.
She forswears perfume,
costly eau de cologne,
trick-essence that wrists bedaub
to fool other spirits.

The cynic in me smells a rat, this is merely
my human need to sniff out a soul.
Still,
I'll stick to my snout,
hot on the scent of the escaped inmate,
caught from shirt or shoe,
bound to be duped again,
left staring bewildered and foolish

across the scentless bank of the widest of rivers.

Snow and Wind Canticle to an Unborn Child

Now the morning snowstorm is a swarm
     of white locusts, not a biblical black wind
devouring all before it, but a charm
     of benign creatures whose seeming simple end
is to becalm, dropping a bright humility
     on the world, bringing the city to a stand-
still, turning their wings into a white sea
     of, when walked on, what sounds like soft sand
that gets piled in snow combers or cotton candy,
     or shaped into a button-eyed, carrot-nosed fatso.
Our plump snowman, whose eyes are still as blind
     as buttons, soon we'll show you this and so
much more; how now what is called wind
     blows a snow kiss, invisible as they say God is.

The Christmas Gift

for Robert Mañuel Ferreira

Patti wraps the last of the presents below.
The paper's got purple Santas, cardinal-red
     bob houses and deer cavorting on yellow snow.
The radio wassails. She won't let me head
     downstairs for fear I'll spot my unwrapped gift.
Don't be miffed
          if she has nothing for you.
          She has one last gift to do.
     I think it's Mona's. Rob, I can't help feeling
               you're still here and wrapping up now too,
struggling with Christmas paper before we arrive, cursing,
          as I do with this word-present to you this year.
Where's the phone? Rob, not to worry, we'll be there
     soon. What occurred a numb year ago
               today, knocked the stuffing
     out of us right enough: a sooty-grey snow
               shrouded a black-suited Santa reining
his black deer over your house, exchanging
               you for a sackful of wrapped gifts
               piling round the tree in grief-drifts.

*

     Surely by now you've written our names on tags?
What did you get me? Thought of you is lift
     enough. Man, yuletide sans you is a bags.
Where art thou? You just slipped out – right? – for a few drags
          and to record the temperature that you check daily,
               jotting it into your diary:
     your divine office to the divinities of climate.
It's nones. That's it. Robert, enjoy your old smoke.
So what if it kills you? – that was Lois. She's in a state.
               Lo Loey's no termagant, but, Man, if you croak
     what'll she do? Christ, the thermometer's broke

or else it's minus sixty. Come in, Robby.
You must be frozen as the balls of a brass monkey.
      Not even a cigarette and modicum of peace
is worth that. Are you – the jetsam of military play –
            back manning your SOS combat-fatigue days,
      diving from the listing *USS Wasp* in war's caprice,
            threading the flaming water, dodging the splay
of strafing, surrounded by buddies picked off by shark,
      floundering among killers in your cellar's dark?

                              *

Who'd have thought the box we'd get you would be such
            a box. For the record, it was made of yew.
      The same grain as the bench
            you were redoing. It didn't cost too much.
It was simple, tidy and lovely
      like yourself. Honestly.
Don't be embarrassed, Rob. Do you hear me? What's new?
      I'm sending you this spirit-post, Pegasus-express.
There's a notion such letters get through
      the impossible security there, another SOS
            vain flare. Come on, send us a clue
                  you're there. Patti asks are you okeydoke
      often and often. Crack another corny joke.
Come down like you did first thing every dawn
      and brew a pot of joe and tune in to the daily news.
The terrible news still goes. Later I'll come down
      to your Mr Joker *Good afternoon*, your blues
            about the world and listen chipper as I never was.
Wear your collar up, gangster-style, as you always did,
      It's cold. I swear we won't ask where you've hid.

The Doppler is a metal detector
        combing the hill for treasure
        that the amiable, vigilant nurse
slides over the icy hummock
of your mother's gel-rimed stomach.

                *

Your pounding heart racing toward us
        is the sound of a train at full throttle,
        the tittupping of a galloping horse,
or lovers in the next room of a motel,
the headboard morse-coding against the wall.

                *

Then there's the static of your grand
        kicking like someone tapping
        a mike, testing before the band
breaks into its hit song.
Our star, we're psyched to sing along.

                *

The graph roll of the monitor, a tail
        curling, records the seismic shocks
        of your quakes on the foetal Richter scale,
radiating from the tectonic plate of your da
rubbing months ago with the hypocentre of your ma.

                *

You're tucked safely as you can be
        beneath the door jamb of your small room,
        our star, train, love wave, treasure & pony.
Now you've gone quiet as a dormouse,
about to bring down your own house.

A storm of tufty snow softly falling is
      white as the God placed on my child tongue,
an O or zero of white, awkward as a kiss,
      set with an Amen, as the choir sung
the Latin canticles, and head bowed,
      hands clasped, I returned to my parents' pew
in my spruce Sunday best, among a hushed loud
      litany of Amens that our God was true
and meek and simple as my own ma and da were,
      innocent as today's verity of perfect snow
is white. Suddenly, amid shut faces, I'm lost somewhere
      beyond the miscount of seats down to our row.
The host, cleaved to my palate, won't come unclung.
I strain to scrape the dissolving God free with my tongue.

Sparrows mostly, but chickadees,
cardinals, finches, wild canaries
feed all day on our bird-house stairs.
Sunflower seeds, beautiful black tears
your father gave us only a year ago.
He is dead now. How were we to know?
Snow is a white sheet laid silently upon
the body of the earth. How the dead live on.

For the Record

Today on Mallet's Bay Avenue I am undone
      by the redivivus of wonder
and not simply by the winter-blade sun
      stirring up the snow's phosphorescence, the under-
iridescence of a pigeon's neck, the jaguar
      in the guise of the svelte street cat.
                            Not simply these,
but the exhaust fuming from a passing car,
      made all the more visible by the freeze
of air, the cumulus of stacks of smoke
      billowing heavenward from McNeil's Generator
and the passing jet drawing a line of coke
      behind it on the sky's blue counter.

Yes, these are not breath or cloud or anything
      to be high on; they are undoing our skies:
the car we drive, the coffee pot plugged in each morning
      and so on and so forth, but it's nothing but lies
not to reiterate how we, the gallinaceous
      species can fly, and make invisible flame,
and draw horseless, elephantless, assless luxurious
      cars and trucks. Give us our due all the same
and so forth and so on: how we somehow manage mostly
      to live together, – confused only by ourselves, our ghostly
genes of fear and survival, too quick to be undone
      by our invention – mad simply to be under the sun.

Child, I'm reduced to playing the amateur masseur,
     quietly desperate, dropping to my knees
to tie your mother's shoes, an obedient chauffeur,
     a bag-lugging coolie eager to ease
your puffed ma as you blow her up like a balloon
     from the inside – yourself within the zeppelin,
dirigible, hot air, gas bag and rocketoon –
     without ever taking a breath, squashing
her innards, forcing her heart to faint
     on its side, her bursting bladder to leak
continually, her crushed lungs to pant
     just at a walk, her spine to bow by the week.
Soon you will become your own cone-headed arrow,
bursting your bubble, dropping into our good morrow.

The Turtle Mother

Your mother is a turtle
stranded on her back,
though with her head
– how distorted, contorted,
discombobulated you have her –
turned the wrong way round,
struggling to get up from bed
or couch, flapping her flippers,
helpless, bewildered, sad,
ancient, determined,
a stranger to herself,
and sometimes somewhat scared
hearing unseen rustlings on the banks
of choked weed, stalking, stalking.
How can a turtle know what dark
predators the day will turn up,
except they are legion? She withdraws
into her shell, your dome and home,
tucked into the thought of you?
Good shell, keep her safe and well.

David points at the two-day snow bunkers along Broadway,
        not the natural jaundiced yellow of melting slush,
but as if a black soot-storm of snow had fallen.
        He remarks how that's what we breathe in every day,
reminding me of how the nuns described the soul
        as a flake of snow and every trespass ash-darkens
that whiteness of whiteness. Ah, the soul of the world
        is made manifest to us today on Broadway and 82nd,
a fuming black exhausted snow-soul, woebegone
        as a bewildered oil-slick bird unable to fly.
I laugh, not without cynicism & apathetic stoicism, qualities
        necessary these days to survive, or rather, to get by.

The Neo-Natal

As the curtain open-sesamed on the glass chests
       of incubators – a dozen or so strewn in the cave
              of natal lights shining above resting neonate –
    I tried not to think of them as the glass-caskets
    of deceased saints or royalty and us as a wave
            of mourners surging up for one last peek,
or worse again, as a kind of freak show
      as we huddled for a gawk,
       though, for all the concerned talk,
somewhere a voice called 'Come up, come up, don't miss
             the smallest babies in the universe.'

They reminded me more of an aquarium
       of black molly, angel, kissing, tiger, butterfly fish…
          seen in a flashy shop or restaurant
             as the winter haunts
windows and doors with blowing ghost-veils of snow.

                *

Incubators covered with white linen
     – protecting the inhabitants from the lights' glow –
          are snug, snow-covered, gambrel-roofed homes
             in miniature, like our own right now,

    or like the shading
         laid over the canary's cage to fool the maestro
           it's night and forty winks time
   – ah, little fledglings, perk up your heads and sing.

*

The nurse draws closed the curtain.
Each child is a magician
      immersed in a glass water tank.
After a breathtaking pause
      may the curtain be unveiled
          and each one be hailed
in a wave of relieved, silent applause.

Arrival

Shades of waiting for a train in India,
      never knowing when it'll show, the dilemma
of having whiled away all curiosity in the other-
      ness of the station: the sacred cow
          humpbacked like a dromedary or your mother
back-to-front; the platform beggars who kowtow
      to the foreigners as yours truly to the doctor;

the lingo, the delivery room's argot that I strain
      to make out; the fear there's no train
even as we hear your distant, unseen express
      pistoning towards us though the monsoon rain
          of monitor static and your mother's distress.
Child, even as we complain you're overdue,
      we crane to catch our first glimpse of you.

The Coronation

Your head settles into the pelvic butterfly
      of your ma. Perhaps it's here the soul penetrates
your potentate's body as you slowly pry
      your way out of your watery, burgeoning state.
You make, at best, a willing but much-pressed
      subject and servant of your loyal queenmother,
what with your tantrums giving her small rest,
      waking her at all hours; and every other
minute ordering her to sit on the throne.
      You've grown fat and despotic, a parody
of a mad medieval king who is prone
      to great and unpredictable cruelty,
and who now, if we look at Your Highness upside down,
      wears our unsettled kingdom's Pelvic Crown.

From Woody's Restaurant, Middlebury

Today, noon, a young macho friendly waiter and three diners,
      business types – two males, one female –
are in a quandary about the name of the duck paddling
      Otter Creek,
the duck being brown, but too large to be a female mallard.
      They really
want to know, and I'm the human-watcher behind the nook
      of my table,
camouflaged by my stillness and nonchalant plumage.
      They really want to know.
This sighting I record in the back of my *Field Guide to People*.

For months your crib is docked waiting for you,
      laden with a shower of gifts:
hand-knit boots with suede soles, mounting drifts
           of rompers, bibs, hats and a slew
           of other offerings laid on your ship of birth
with the ark story embroidered all about.

In this berth the creatures have mostly mirth-
      ful faces: the cachinnating chickadees, the stout stoat,
      the grinning elephant trunk-bailing the boat,
      the droll owl, the odd rainbow trout,
      the one-humped camel you might think is pregnant
          on its back, the polar bear yodelling upon
              a melting green berg, the avuncular ant,
not to speak of the circus of unrecorded creatures on
      your kid attire. Is this saying, unbeknownst to us,
that we gather around the baby
      The Great Circus of the Earth:
          the flying hippopotamus,
          the foetus-like manatee, the dork stork,
          the delirious giraffe…
              not just for a sappy laugh,
but to illuminate their dearth
and our sapien dodo-ing as we fish-mouth sorry
sorrysorrysorrysorrysorrysorry…?

Our little lambkin, waxwing, luckling…
      all the cordial choir are Noah-calling you now:
the lovelice, the leech of paradise, the how-now-down-cow,
the Forever Gone Bird, the Dolly sheep, the flying
kiwi, the crying with laughter jackass, the pronghorn,
the bristleless porcupine, the schizophrenic platypus,
          the liquorice-black crow, the rhinoceros:
            that ancestor of the unicorn
              with an overgrown thorn-horn.

Listen the horns, the horns are blowing,
trumpeting you, our dear humacorn,
beckoning you onto the ark
           out of your first watery dark.
'Hurry now, Hurry now' baritones the polar bear
           'Our icebergs are melting out here.'
'Quick Quick,' the duck sections quack.
           'Darn, darn,'
basso-bleats the goat, stomping time with his hoof
           as the chorus raises the roof:
'All aboard, all aboard, our poor wee bairn.'

A Circus

I doubt anyone would've blinked if a ringmaster
marched in among us and this blarneying broadcaster
raised a megaphone to his lips, announcing
another highlight of the Greatest Show on Earth
along with the likes of the ball-bouncing,
baby-blubber seals; the hoop-leaping lemurs of mirth;
the tremendous, stupendous fandango of horses;
highflying doctors; funambulist nurses;
and all the farraginous farrago of this Earth,
not excluding me, the whistle-blowing clown,
the huffing and puffing red-faced Bozo father
of fathers, wearing a lugubrious frown,
cracking side-splitting sideshow banter
and flat-footed jokes, a sidekick to your mother.
The whole death-defying show spun out of order
as a drum roll hailed you: the debonair,
high-flying, dare-devil, god of the air,
none other than the Cannonball Kid himself
shot from the dilatory, dilative distaff
opening of your ma, the human cannon herself,
lit a little over nine months ago by your father.
Your grey jump suit was smeared with bloody gauze
as you landed in the hand-net of nurse and doctor;
the whole show agape in the pause before applause.

To My Mother

You took a deep breath. It was by what we weren't told
we were told. You sidestepped our questions, big-talked of how cold
the winter was, how there was still a test
to come in. 'Everything will turn out for the best,
please God.' Not till your grandchild was a month old,
not wanting to spoil his entry into the fold,
did you tell us the cancer'd got you buttonholed,
casual, as if it was just a troublesome guest.
      It took your breath,
the rampant cell's stranglehold
on your alveoli, the invaded hold
of your spiritus. Your chest
tightened even as the child's spirit lodged in him. You didn't protest,
consoled by him, you prayed, please God, it could be controlled,
      not turn out a breath for a breath.

The Ink Moth

Introducing Seamus Heaney at the first Katharine Washburn Translation Memorial

Remember our path crossed the gloaming fall path
      of *Isia Isabella*, the woolly
            bear caterpillar? You called it the furry bear.

You remarked, in between fortifying belles-lettres chat
      agus craic,
how you hadn't laid eyes on one in donkey's years.
      Not since, I figured, back
            in the pupa ground of our own country.

The bog brown & black mite
– a wee concertina or bellows – traversed our drive's tarmac
          as sails beyond on the lake luffed,
      white moth wings in cuff-white wave tuft.
Someone unseen and unknown laughed,
      a lovely Lucullan disembodied laugh, breeze-lilted
           around the corner of Lake View Terrace and Berry

as Patti welcomed you, her belly a spinnaker
      swelling with the wind, the zephyr,
         of our first miteling fluttering in her.

Such a luculent moment has stayed with me. You predicting
      a boy, vatic as the woolly bear
         forecasting winter.
Both of you were right, the winter being severe,
        though not for us,
     and the boy is a reality of flesh
         and bone as I coax from pupae inklings
            this ink moth.

*

Somewhere the woolly bear
          opens. To call it the furry bear
                    is nearer eye-truth,
it resembling a miniature dowager's stole worn
to the opera, or some literary hobnobbing shindig. But where
                    is Katharine?
She'd be in her element here.

Her company like yours, Seamus,
          was the spring touch that released in us
                    the woolly bear moth,

the love moth I translate it to here,
          stuttering into the air, into the air
          winging it here and here
                              and here.

The Language of Crying

We're still learning the language of crying,
its parent-boggling irregular grammar.
To hear you now you'd think you were dying.

Puzzling gerunds beyond the clarifying
syllables of raw hunger's regular yammer.
We're still learning the language of crying.

Diaper-changed we take turns rock-a-bying,
bawling at each other please please be calmer.
To hear you now you'd think you were dying:

a demented king's yowling, terrifying
soliloquy beyond a royal diaper-rash clamour.
We're still learning the language of crying.

Christ child, such a caterwaul's parent-petrifying,
hardly a put on, you're no shammer.
To hear you now you'd think you were dying.

Is it something you sense? A wordless prophesying?
Surely the future's not teething yet. We stammer.
We're still learning the language of crying.
To hear you now you'd think you were dying.

The Road Hazard

Nothing but the quick fix, the narcotic of the car,
    relieved you and us from your long caterwaul,
        an option we've resisted so far.
But tonight, short on the wherewithal
    of energy and sleep, we strapped you into
        the car seat's straitjacket, you waking all
            the neighbours. You were sound by North Avenue.
I got the feeling that the highways
    and byways, in the small hours, streamed with a steady dream
        of rookie parents whispering, second-guessing if it's okay
            to sneak home now; those drivers who seem
    to be alone, telling herself or himself not to keep
glancing back at their cradled road hazard for one last peep,
    and not simply to see if their sleep-depriver is asleep.

Posthalamion

to a newly married couple

The snow which doth the top of Pindus strew,
Did never whiter shew…
               Edmund Spenser, 'Prothalamion'

Today the snow takes the shape of the world,
      having shimmied and trembled in the air
           all night as you slept snow-curled,
flake-furled into each other without fear
      for once, of what befalls outside
           your window as if you yourself inside
made the snow fall out of inner air
      confetti-ing the night in a beneficence
           of swan down, keeping souls from the graveyard,
becoming silence
      made visible. And yes, you know it's hard
           on some bird or some poor soul barred outside,
but for now you two are without a doubt
      that the world in the window-shard of your yard
           is bright. The wedding-veil snow,
gossamer-light, in the shape of the shed, car, bobsleigh
and frozen lake, takes the shushed aspect of all you know.
And looking across the whitened bay,
      you recall some deity
           laying himself down across the waterway,
allowing a brace of mortals to cross over in certain safety.

Shades of the green room about this scenario.
You lounge beneath the drip of the chemo,
Talking shop with others, some bald, some still blest
With their own mops of hair, making the best
Of your body's flaw and a visitor's melodrama.
You slip in and of out your latest part: the nausea,
Dry mouth, diarrhoea, the poison's impact,
Having to go back out and face the next act.
The nurse assures you that you look just fine
Even in your wig, that you're eternally twenty-nine.
You perk up, introduce 'My son, the poet' to everyone.
A bald lady asks me, 'Do your poems rhyme like that one
Fear no more the heat o' the sun – we did in school?
Write us one like that.' 'Okeydoke,' says I, playing the fool.

Chemotherapy

The I.V. bag hangs from the coat rack
of the stand – the revealed trick
up the sleeve
of the doctor, wizard, white-coated necromancer
who would have you believe
that this bag of what
appears to be no more than water
will save you.

Centre stage,
you sit and chat
– what can you do? –
surrounded by relatives and nurses. You're invincible as Rasputin,
forecasting the future,
feeding yourself doses of transparent poison,
outmanoeuvering your disloyal cells' rampage.

A few more treatments and you're through.
You gag.
The nurse peps
you up with banter.
She clips on a fresh drip bag
bulging like a strongman's flexed biceps.

The Cough

Your mother lays you swaddled into my arms,
        her lips pursed, miming
                shush, you being in the charms
                        of sleep, a balm for us after the alarms
                        of your latest bout of cryptic crying.
I carry you upstairs with the step by
        tentative step of an explosives expert
        handling nitroglycerine,
                        or like myself as I
snuck upstairs, the typical rebel, my heart
        in my teenage mouth, my concocted excuses turning
                cornier on each creaky step, listening
                for a stir, slipping
        inside the sheets, only to hear my father cough,
his love-worry cough, more admonishing than any telling off.

Fontanelle

It wasn't until ruffling the tomentose
      of your dark hair and making a gentle tom-
            tom of your head that I felt it. My hand froze
    on the round, soft membrane of your dome.
I must have looked like doubting Thomas
      tentatively touching the unbelievable hole,
          the terrifying recess,
    withdrawing my hand from your poll,
the cerebrum beneath your skull, beneath everything,
      my eyes touch on: the cup, tea, prayer plant, book,
          trees in the window, the window, the workers painting
    across the road, the paint, the shimmering rook…
Now as your parietal bone shuts tight as a walnut,
    I excuse this as tomfoolery and myself a nut.

You took such care of your hair.
      Now it comes out in clumps. 'Maybe
            my new grandson could spare
                a share,'
you joked, Barber Death breathing down your neck.
Always joking we are, keeping something or other in check,
        the Joker Family.

Remember how we'd beg you to open the window
      of our grey, white-topped Ford Anglia? But no,
      a mere hairline window crack of in-rushing air
         would toss your hair.
How we sweltered on those eternal drives to Everywhere:
Fountainstown, Ringabella, Redbarn, Castlegregory, Glenbeigh.

'Now look at the scenery while the weather's fine,' you'd say,
'We'll stop soon and each have a 99,' fixing your hair
        in the rear
view mirror in that special way.
Ma, any chance of a bit of air?

                *

Lately, on a drive round the Ring, near Kenmare,
      I risked wisecracking how your wig
is almost as good as your own erstwhile hair,
          itself a look-alike periwig,
and that, at least, we can open the car window.
      How we all laughed – you also.
      How the winds blow.

It's a bit like the rhododendron in Kerry
flourishing west above the lakes all the way
      to Derrynane, the wilder purple kind, beautiful
in itself, yes, beguiling, overshadowing
      quieter plants, not seeing how the rhodo
winds its way around and over the native seedlings
      of ash, oak, holly, hazel, fern,
climbing their backs, suffocating them, shutting out light,
      spreading, spreading, spreading; cutting ancient links
in the great chain: the insects, birds, animals,
      even the rare deer of these parts, barring its gentle way.
Still, we're taken by this purple fantasy,
      forgetting the nightmare beneath the flower,
the dreadful root and stem-tendril arms
      that even when cut back, gain ground,
squeezing the life out of undergrowth,
      the under-strata of our shaded wood.

The Wave

I slip away
        – never being a morning person, Ma, as you say –
leaving you, seemingly crisp as fresh cornflakes,
playing peekaboo with Dan. He can't find you.
        Peekaboopeekaboo.
             For heaven's sakes,
             You're putting a good face on things. Fair dues.
Even if you don't quite know the test's full news.
        Ma, I think you know.
        How can we say your body is coming apart?
Sure, aren't we all anyway. Ah, have a heart.

A boat is shouldered like a coffin across the dunes off Lamb's Head.

        Where do you go when you're dead?
Remember I'd pester you about that, not much older than Danno?

Already you're making ready.
We watch from above. Your boat bobs insecurely.
Run up the sail. Let me give you a hand. Show.
It's so clear on the horizon today
        and the water so calm beyond the bay.
You head out beyond Bird Island towards Teach Duinn.
        A quick getaway would be a boon.
        Dan has learned to wave now too.
             He'll never remember you.
Look Ma, my hand. You'll be out of sight soon.

The Birds

At dinner a friend admired the regular birds at our feeder:
the seal-sleek grackles, the rouged house finch,
the natty chickadees, the tan mourning doves.
She asks, being a bird lover, if we'd unusual ones of late.
I mentioned the cowbirds of today. She made a face,
explained to the company how the cowbird is worse
than any Old World cuckoo, laying eggs in a wider range
of foster birds' nests, the cowfledgling killing the other brood.
As others at the table grimaced, I admitted a fondness
for the cowbird, this cowboy in the brown hood,
who, according to bird-heads, are thus since following
bison across the plains, without any time to nest.
What else could these uprooted creatures do? We survive rightly
or wrongly. And who are we to talk, us American flock?
The birds might ask – even the cowbird – who is
any person to talk? Where are the great bison herds now?
Ah, don't be so hard on the cowbirds.
They're simply caught up in old ways. And, besides,
I like their silly finch-beaks stuck on their crow heads
like those characters in that Greek comedy
about a better world, with bird beaks stuck on their pates.
Yes, like one of those characters in a Greek comedy.

The Skunk Moths

The family of skunks, their backs to me from our deck,
       are like great black & white caterpillars. I imagine them
the giant larvae of Luna moths or Monarch butterflies,
       their pupae unzipping and tremendous wings
unfolding, fluttering about the summer airways, big as people.
       And why not? I think we'd be frightened of such creatures,
each's revanchist proboscis, exacting retribution for the legions
       we've not let flutter down the summers? Imagine
their great eyes, big as cow eyes, gazing, gazing, gazing at us.
       Imagine the Luna's gossamer tulle wings, the tippets
brushing us, fanning us tenderly, wrapping us in a veil,
       bringing us gently to our knees in a gathering humility,
brushing aside our mortification, finally at home, natural
       in the natural world – their wings our cocoon – becoming
ourselves, pinioned resplendence, at last the human mothfly.

Late Entry

The white sea of a record storm was just ploughed open;
      great snow combers were held back either side of the road.
There was the quality of the miraculous about the night,
      a crossing over out of danger, a leavetaking
and an arrival. While your ma zipped the overnight bag, I swabbed
      the breaking-waters that could have been spilt tea
on the lino of our kitchen floor. I pulled the car round
      to the front, helping her in as a hooded figure
scavenged our recycle bin, our poor attempt to save the world.
      I wanted to call out, say there's no need to scurry
away, a modern-day leper, but another spasm
      of your overdue entry had me behind the wheel
and us off, only to be flagged down on Pearl Street
      by a police road block. Two streets later a driver
in a blizzard of alcohol barred the way, refused
      to allow us pass until his girlfriend implored him.
On making the hospital the monitoring nurse assured us
      you'd probably slept through it all: the groaning,
the shopping cart's leper-rattle, the swarming police
      brisk in the drama of god-knows-what crime,
the drunken man's swearing and so much I've forgotten
      or totally missed in the white-out of your storming.